The Mahabharata Of Krishna-Dwaipayana Vyasa

Vol. 4, Book 16,17,18

by

Kisari Mohan Ganguli

Double9 BOOKS

The Mahabharata of Krishna-Dwaipayana Vyasa

VOl. 4, BOOK 16,17,18

by Kisari Mohan Ganguli

ISBN: 978-93-58595-47-5

Published by

DOUBLE 9 BOOKS

2/13-B, Ansari Road
Daryaganj, New Delhi – 110002
info@double9books.com
www.double9books.com
Tel. 011-40042856

ABOUT THE AUTHOR

The Sanskrit epic Mahabharata was translated into English for the first time by Kisari Mohan Ganguli (also known as K. M. Ganguli), an Indian translator. The Mahabharata of Krishna-Dwaipayana Vyasa, the product of his translation, was released. Between 1883 and 1896, Pratap Chandra Roy (1842-1955), a bookseller in Calcutta who owned a printing press and gathered money for the undertaking, translated the work into English prose.

CONTENTS

BOOK 16
Mausala-parva

1

Om! Having bowed down unto Narayana, and to Nara, the foremost of men, as also to the goddess Sarasvati, should the word "Jaya" be uttered.

"Vaishampayana said: 'When the thirty-sixth year (after the battle) was reached, the delighter of the Kurus, Yudhishthira, beheld many unusual portents. Winds, dry and strong, and showering gravels, blew from every side. Birds began to wheel, making circles from right to left. The great rivers ran in opposite directions. The horizon on every side seemed to be always covered with fog. Meteors, showering (blazing) coals, fell on the Earth from the sky. The Sun's disc, O king, seemed to be always covered with dust. At its rise, the great luminary of day was shorn of splendour and seemed to be crossed by headless trunks (of human beings). Fierce circles of light were seen every day around both the Sun and the Moon. These circles showed three hues. Their edges seemed to be black and rough and ashy-red in colour. These and many other omens, foreshadowing fear and danger, were seen, O king, and filled the hearts of men with anxiety. A little while after, the Kuru king Yudhishthira heard of the wholesale carnage of the Vrishnis in consequence of the iron bolt. The son of Pandu, hearing that only Vasudeva and Rama had escaped with life, summoned his brothers and took counsel with them as to what they should do. Meeting with one another, they became greatly distressed upon hearing that the Vrishnis had met with destruction through the Brahmana's rod of chastisement. The death of Vasudeva, like the drying up of the ocean, those heroes could not believe. In fact the destruction of the wielder of Saranga was incredible to them. Informed of the incident about the iron bolt, the Pandavas became filled with grief and sorrow. In fact, they sat down, utterly cheerless and penetrated with blank despair.'

"Janamejaya said: 'Indeed, O holy one, how was it that the Andhakas along with Vrishnis, and those great car-warriors, the Bhojas, met with destruction in the very sight of Vasudeva?'

"Vaishampayana continued: 'When the thirty-sixth year was reached (after the great battle) a great calamity overtook the Vrishnis. Impelled by Time, they all met with destruction in consequence of the iron bolt.'

"Janamejaya said: 'Cursed by whom did those heroes, the Vrishnis, the Andhakas, and the Bhojas, met with destruction? O foremost of regenerate persons, do thou tell me this in detail.'

"Vaishampayana continued: 'One day, the Vrishni heroes numbering Samva amongst them, saw Vishvamitra and Kanwa and Narada arrived at Dwaraka. Afflicted by the rod of chastisement wielded by the deities, those heroes, causing Samva to be disguised like a woman, approached those ascetics and said, "This one is the wife of Vabhru of immeasurable energy who is desirous of having a son. Ye Rishis, do you know for certain what this one will bring forth?"

"'Hear now, O king, what those ascetics, attempted to be thus deceived, said: "This heir of Vasudeva, by name Samva, will bring forth a fierce iron bolt for the destruction of the Vrishnis and the Andhakas. Ye wicked and cruel ones, intoxicated with pride, through that iron bolt ye will become the exterminators of your race with the exception of Rama and Janarddana. The blessed hero armed with the plough will enter the ocean, casting off his body, while a hunter of the name of Jara will pierce the high-souled Krishna while lying on the ground."

"'Endeavoured to be deceived by those wicked ones, those ascetics, with eyes red in wrath, looked at each other and uttered those words. Having said so they then proceeded to see Keshava. The slayer of Madhu, informed of what had taken place, summoned all the Vrishnis and told them of it. Possessed of great intelligence and fully acquainted with what the end of his race would be, he simply said that that which was destined would surely happen. Hrishikesa having said so, entered his mansion. The Lord of the universe did not wish to ordain otherwise. When the next day came, Samva actually brought forth an iron bolt through which all the individuals in the race of the Vrishnis and the Andhakas became consumed into ashes. Indeed, for the destruction of the Vrishnis and the Andhakas, Samva brought forth, through that curse, a fierce iron bolt that looked like a gigantic messenger of death. The fact was duly reported to the king. In great distress of mind, the king (Ugrasena) caused that iron bolt to be reduced into fine powder. Men were employed, O king, to cast that powder into the sea. At the command of Ahuka, of Janarddana, of Rama, and of the high-souled Vabhru, it was, again, proclaimed throughout the city that from that day, among all the Vrishnis and the Andhakas no one should manufacture wines and intoxicating spirits of any kind, and that whoever would secretly manufacture wines and spirits should be impaled alive with all his kinsmen. Through fear of the king, and knowing that it was the command of Rama also of unimpeachable deeds, all the citizens bound themselves by a rule and abstained from manufacturing wines and spirits.'"

2

"Vaishampayana said: 'While the Vrishnis and the Andhakas were thus endeavouring (to avoid the impending calamity), the embodied form of Time (death) every day wandered about their houses. He looked like a man of terrible and fierce aspect. Of bald head, he was black and of tawny complexion. Sometimes he was seen by the Vrishnis as he peered into their houses. The mighty bowmen among the Vrishnis shot hundreds and thousands of shafts at him, but none of these succeeded in piercing him, for he was none else than the Destroyer of all creatures. Day by day strong winds blew, and many were the evil omens that arose, awful and foreboding the destruction of the Vrishnis and the Andhakas. The streets swarmed with rats and mice. Earthen pots showed cracks or broke from no apparent cause. At night, the rats and mice ate away the hair and nails of slumbering men. Sarikas chirped, sitting within the houses of the Vrishnis. The noise made by those birds ceased not for even a short while by day or by night. The Sarashas were heard to imitate the hooting of the owl, and goats imitated the cries, O Bharata, of jackals. Many birds appeared, impelled by Death, that were pale of complexion but that had legs red of hue. Pigeons were seen to always disport in the houses of the Vrishnis. Asses were born of kine, and elephants of mules. Cats were born of bitches, and mouse of the mongoose. The Vrishnis, committing sinful acts, were not seen to feel any shame. They showed disregard for Brahmanas and the Pitris and the deities. They insulted and humiliated their preceptors and seniors. Only Rama and Janardana acted differently. Wives deceived their husbands, and husbands deceived their wives. Fires, when ignited, cast their flames towards the left. Sometimes they threw out flames whose splendour was blue and red. The Sun, whether when rising or setting over the city, seemed to be surrounded by headless trunks of human form. In cook rooms, upon food that was clean and well-boiled, were seen, when it was served out for eating, innumerable worms of diverse kinds. When Brahmanas, receiving gifts, blessed the day or the hour (fixed for this or that undertaking) or when high-souled men were engaged in silent recitations, the heavy tread was heard of innumerable men running about, but no one could be seen to whom the sound of such tread could be ascribed. The constellations were repeatedly seen to be struck by the planets. None amongst the Yadavas could, however, obtain a sight of the constellation of his birth. When the Panchajanya was blown in their houses, asses of dissonant and awful voice brayed aloud from every direction. Beholding these signs that indicated the perverse course of Time, and seeing that the day of the new moon coincided with the thirteenth (and the fourteenth) lunation, Hrishikesa, summoning the Yadavas, said unto them these words: "The fourteenth lunation has been made the fifteenth by Rahu once more. Such a day had happened at the time of the great battle of the Bharatas. It has once more appeared, it seems, for our destruction." The slayer of Keshi, Janardana, thinking upon the omens that Time showed, understood that the thirty-sixth year had come, and that what Gandhari, burning with grief on account of the death of her sons, and deprived of all her kinsmen, had said was about to transpire. "The present is exactly similar to that time when Yudhishthira noted at such awful omens when the two armies had been arrayed in order of battle." Vasudeva, having said so, endeavoured to bring about those occurrences which would make Gandhari's words true. That chastiser of foes commanded the Vrishnis to make a pilgrimage to some sacred water. The messengers forthwith proclaimed at the command of Keshava that the Vrishnis should make a journey to the sea-coast for bathing in the sacred waters of the ocean.'"

3

"Vaishampayana said: 'At that time the Vrishni ladies dreamed every night that a woman of black complexion and white teeth, entering their abodes, laughed aloud and ran through Dwaraka, snatching from them the auspicious threads in their wrists. The men dreamt that terrible vultures, entering their houses and fire-chambers, gorged themselves on their bodies. Their ornaments and umbrellas and standards and armour were seen to be taken away by terrible Rakshasas. In the very sight of the Vrishnis, the discus of Krishna, given by Agni, made of iron and having its nave composed of hardest adamant, ascended into the firmament. In the very sight of Daruka, the excellent car of Vasudeva, of solar effulgence, and properly equipped, was taken away by the horses yoked unto it. Those foremost of steeds, numbering four, (Saivya, Sugriva, Meghapushpa and Valahaka), and endued with the speed of thought, fled away, dragging the car after them along the surface of the ocean. The two great standards of Krishna's car and Valadeva's car, that with the device of Garuda and that bearing the device of the palmyra, which were reverently worshipped by those two heroes, were taken away by Apsaras who, day and night, called upon the Vrishnis and the Andhakas to set out on a pilgrimage to some sacred water. When these omens were seen and heard, those foremost of men, the mighty car-warriors of the Vrishnis and the Andhakas, became desirous of setting out, with their whole families, on a pilgrimage to some sacred water. They prepared diverse kinds of viands and edibles and diverse kinds of wines and meat. The troops of the Vrishnis and the Andhakas, blazing with beauty and endued with fierce energy, then set out from the city on cars and steeds and elephants. The Yadavas, then, with their wives, proceeded to Prabhasa and took up their residence there, each in the (temporary) habitation that was assigned to him, and all having an abundance of provisions consisting of edibles and drink.

"'Hearing that they had taken up their abode on the sea-coast, Uddhava, the wisest of men, who was, besides, well-versed in Yoga, proceeded there and took his leave (for departing). Krishna, with joined hands, saluted Uddhava, and seeing him bent on departing (from the world) and knowing that the destructions of the Vrishnis was at hand, did not feel any disposition to prevent him. The mighty car-warriors among the Vrishnis and the Andhakas, whose hour had come, then saw Uddhava proceed on his great journey, filling the whole welkin with his splendour. The Vrishnis, mixing with wine the food that had been cooked for high-souled Brahmanas, gave it away unto monkeys and apes. Those heroes of fierce energy then began their high revels, of which drinking formed the chief feature, at Prabhasa. The entire field echoed with the blare of hundreds of trumpets and abounded with actors and dancers plying their vocations. In the very sight of Krishna, Rama began to drink, with Kritavarma, Yuyudhana and Gada; and Vabhru also did the same. Then Yuyudhana, inebriated with wine, derisively laughing at and insulting Kritavarma in the midst of that assembly, said, "What Kshatriya is there who, armed with weapons, will slay men locked in the embraces of sleep and, therefore, already dead? Hence, O son of Hridika, the Yadavas will never tolerate what thou hast done." When Yuyudhana had said these words, Pradyumna, that foremost of car-warriors, applauded them, expressing his disregard for the son of Hridika.

"'Highly incensed at this, Kritavarma, emphasising his disregard for Satyaki, by pointing to him with his left hand, said these words: "Professing thyself to be a hero, how couldst thou so cruelly slay the armless Bhurishrava who, on the field of battle, (gave up all hostile intentions and) sat in praya?"

"'Hearing these words of his, Keshava, that slayer of hostile heroes, giving way to wrath, cast an angry glance at Kritavarma. Then Satyaki informed the slayer of Madhu as to how Kritavarma had behaved towards Satrajit for taking away from him the celebrated gem Syamantaka. Hearing the narrative, Satyabhama, giving way to wrath and tears, approached Keshava and sitting on his lap enhanced his anger (for Kritavarma). Then rising up in a rage, Satyaki said, "I swear to thee by Truth that I shall soon cause this one to follow in the wake of the five sons of Draupadi, and of Dhrishtadyumna and Shikhandi, they that were slain by this sinful wretch, while they were asleep, with the assistance of Drona's son. O thou of slender waist, Kritavarma's period of life and fame have come to their end."

"'Having said these words, Satyaki rushed at Kritavarma and severed his head with a sword in the very sight of Keshava. Yuyudhana, having achieved this feat, began to strike down others there present. Hrishikesa ran to prevent him from doing further mischief. At that time, however, O monarch, the Bhojas and Andhakas, impelled by the perverseness of the hour that had come upon them, all became as one man and surrounded the son of Sini. Janardana of mighty energy, knowing the character of the hour, stood unmoved without giving way to anger at the sight of those heroes rushing in wrath at Satyaki from every side. Urged by fate and inebriated with drink, they began to strike Yuyudhana with the pots from which they had been eating. When the son of Sini was being thus assaulted, Rukmini's son became highly enraged. He rushed forward for rescuing Satyaki who was engaged with the Bhojas and the Andhakas. Endued with might of arms and wealth of energy, those two heroes exerted themselves with great courage. But as the odds were overwhelming, both of them were slain in the very sight of Krishna. The delighter of the Yadus, beholding his own son, and the son of Sini too, slain, took up, in wrath, a handful of the Eraka grass that grew there. That handful of grass became a terrible bolt of iron endued with the energy of the thunderbolt. With it Krishna slew all those that came before him. Then the Andhakas and the Bhojas, the Saineyas and the Vrishnis, urged by Time, struck one another in that fearful melee. Indeed, O king, whoever amongst them took up in wrath a few blades of the Eraka grass, these, in his hands, became soon converted into a thunderbolt, O puissant one. Every blade of grass there was seen to be converted into a terrible iron bolt. All this, know, O king, was due to the curse denounced by Brahmanas. He who hurled a blade of grass saw that it pierced through even such things as were utterly impenetrable. In fact, every blade was seen to become a terrible bolt having the force of thunder. Son killed sire, and sire killed son, O Bharata. Inebriated with wine, they rushed and fell upon one another. The Kukuras and the Andhakas met with destruction like insects rushing at a blazing fire. As they were thus being slaughtered, no one among them thought of escaping by flight. Knowing that the hour of destruction had come, the mighty-armed Keshava stood there, eyeing everything. Indeed, the slayer of Madhu stood, raising a bolt of iron formed of a blade of grass. Beholding that Samva was slain, as also Charudeshna and Pradyumna and Aniruddha, Madhava became filled with rage. Beholding Gada lying dead on the ground, his wrath became enhanced. The wielder of Sarnga and the discus and the mace then exterminated the Vrishnis and the Andhakas. Hear, O king, what that conquerer of hostile towns, Vabhru of mighty energy and Daruka then said to Krishna, "O holy one, a very large number of men has been slain by thee. Turn now to where Rama has gone. We wish to go there where he has proceeded."'"

4

"Vaishampayana said: 'Then Daruka and Keshava and Vabhru left that spot, following in the wake of Rama (for discovering his retreat). They beheld that hero of infinite energy sitting thoughtfully, reclining his back against a tree, in a solitary spot of earth. Finding Rama of great soul, Krishna commanded Daruka, saying, "Going to the Kurus, inform Partha of this great slaughter of the Yadus. Let Arjuna come here quickly, hearing of the destruction of the Yadavas through the Brahmana's curse."

"'Thus addressed, Daruka, deprived of his senses by grief, proceeded on a car to the (capital of the) Kurus. After Daruka had gone away, Keshava, seeing Vabhru waiting on him, told him these words: "Do thou go quickly for protecting the ladies. Let not robbers do them any injury, tempted by the wealth (that is with them)." Thus commanded by Keshava, Vabhru, still helpless with wine but cheerless at the slaughter of his kinsmen, departed. He had rested for a while by the side of Keshava, but as soon as he had proceeded to a distance, the iron-bolt, attaching itself to a mallet in the hands of a hunter, suddenly sprang of itself upon that solitary survivor of the Yadava race and slew him, who also had been included in the curse of the Brahmanas. Beholding Vabhru slain, Keshava of great energy addressed his elder brother and said, "Do thou, O Rama wait for me here till I place the ladies under the care of kinsmen."

"'Entering the city of Dwaravati, Janardana said these words unto his father, "Do thou protect all the ladies of our house, till Dhananjaya comes. At the skirts of the forest Rama is waiting for me. I shall meet him today. This great carnage of the Yadus has been beheld by me even as I beheld before the carnage of those Kshatriyas who were the foremost ones of Kuru's race. It is impossible for me to see this city of the Yadavas without the Yadus beside me. Know that proceeding to the woods I shall practise penances with Rama in my company." Having said these words, Krishna touched the feet of his father with his head, and quickly left his presence. Then a loud wail of sorrow arose from the ladies and children of his house. Hearing that loud sound of wailing uttered by the weeping ladies, Keshava retraced his foot-steps and said unto them, "Arjuna will come here. That foremost of men will relieve you of your grief."

"'Proceeding then to the forest, Keshava beheld Rama sitting in a solitary spot thereof. He also saw that Rama had set himself to Yoga and that from out his mouth was issuing a mighty snake. The colour of that snake was white. Leaving the human body (in which he had dwelt so long), that high-souled naga of a 1,000 heads and having a form as large as that of a mountain, endued besides with red eyes, proceeded along that way which led to the ocean. Ocean himself, and many celestial snakes, and many sacred Rivers were there, for receiving him with honour. There were Karkotaka and Vasuki and Takshaka and Prithusravas and Varuna and Kunjara, and Misri and Sankha and Kumuda and Pundarika, and the high-souled Dhritarashtra, and Hrada and Kratha and Sitikantha of fierce energy, and Chakramanda and Atishanda, and that foremost of Nagas called Durmukha, and Amvarisha, and king Varuna himself, O monarch. Advancing forward and offering him the Arghya and water to wash his feet, and with diverse other rites, they all worshipped the mighty Naga and saluted him by making the usual enquiries.

"'After his brother had thus departed from the (human) world, Vasudeva of celestial vision, who was fully acquainted with the end of all things, wandered for some time in that lonely forest thoughtfully. Endued with great energy he then sat down on the bare earth. He had thought before this of everything that had been fore-shadowed by the words uttered by Gandhari in former days. He also recollected the words that Durvasas had spoken at the time his body was smeared by that Rishi with the remnant of the Payasa he had eaten (while a guest at Krishna's house). The high-souled one, thinking of the destruction of the Vrishnis and the Andhakas, as also of the previous slaughter of the Kurus, concluded that the hour (for his own departure from the world) had come. He then restrained his senses (in Yoga). Conversant with the truth of every topic, Vasudeva, though he was the Supreme Deity, wished to die, for dispelling all doubts and establishing a certainty of results (in the matter of human existence), simply for upholding the three worlds and for making the words of Atri's son true. Having restrained all his senses, speech, and mind, Krishna laid himself down in high Yoga.

"'A fierce hunter of the name of Jara then came there, desirous of deer. The hunter, mistaking Keshava, who was stretched on the earth in high Yoga, for a deer, pierced him at the heel with a shaft and quickly came to that spot for capturing his prey. Coming up, Jara beheld a man dressed in yellow robes, rapt in Yoga and endued with many arms. Regarding himself an offender, and filled with fear, he touched the feet of Keshava. The high-souled one comforted him and then ascended upwards, filling the entire welkin with splendour. When he reached Heaven, Vasava and the twin Ashvinis and Rudra and the Adityas and the Vasus and the Viswedevas, and Munis and Siddhas and many foremost ones among the Gandharvas, with the Apsaras, advanced to receive him. Then, O king, the illustrious Narayana of fierce energy, the Creator and Destroyer of all, that preceptor of Yoga, filling Heaven with his splendour, reached his own inconceivable region. Krishna then met the deities and (celestial) Rishis and Charanas, O king, and the foremost ones among the Gandharvas and many beautiful Apsaras and Siddhas and Saddhyas. All of them, bending in humility, worshipped him. The deities all saluted him, O monarch, and many foremost of Munis and Rishis worshipped him who was the Lord of all. The Gandharvas waited on him, hymning his praises, and Indra also joyfully praised him.'"

5

"Vaishampayana said: 'Meanwhile Daruka, going to the Kurus and seeing those mighty car-warriors, the son of Pritha, informed them of how the Vrishnis had slain one another with iron bolts. Hearing that the Vrishnis along with the Bhojas and Andhakas and Kukuras had all been slain, the Pandavas, burning with grief, became highly agitated. Then Arjuna, the dear friend of Keshava, bidding them farewell, set out for seeing his maternal uncle. He said that destruction would soon overtake everything. Proceeding to the city of the Vrishnis with Daruka in his company, O puissant king, that hero beheld that the city of Dwaraka looked like a woman bereft of her husband. Those ladies who had, before this, the very Lord of the universe for their protector, were now lordless. Seeing that Partha had come for protecting them, they all set up a loud wail. 16,000 ladies had been wedded to Vasudeva. Indeed, as soon as they saw Arjuna arrive, they uttered a loud cry of sorrow. As soon as the Kuru prince met those beauteous ones deprived of the protection of Krishna and of their sons as well, he was unable to look at them, his vision being obstructed by tears. The Dwaraka river had the Vrishnis and the Andhakas for its water, steeds for its fishes, cars for its rafts, the sound of musical instruments and the rattle of cars for its waves, houses and mansions and public squares for its lakes. Gems and precious stones were its abundant moss. The walls of adamant were the garlands of flowers that floated on it. The streets and roads were the strong currents running in eddies along its surface. The great open squares were the still large lakes in its course. Rama and Krishna were its two mighty alligators. That agreeable river now seemed to Arjuna to be the fierce Vaitarani bound up with Time's net. Indeed, the son of Vasava, endued with great intelligence, beheld the city to look even thus, reft as it was of the Vrishni heroes. Shorn of beauty, and perfectly cheerless, it presented the aspect of a lotus flower in the season of winter. Beholding the sight that Dwaraka presented, and seeing the numerous wives of Krishna, Arjuna wailed aloud with eyes bathed in tears and fell down on the earth. Then Satya, the daughter of Satrajit, and Rukmini too, O king, fell down beside Dhananjaya and uttered loud wails of grief. Raising him then they caused him to be seated on a golden seat. The ladies sat around that high-souled one, giving expression to their feelings. Praising Govinda and talking with the ladies, the son of Pandu comforted them and then proceeded to see his maternal uncle.'"

6

"Vaishampayana said: 'The Kuru prince beheld the heroic and high-souled Anakadundubhi lying on the ground and burning with grief on account of his sons. The broad-chested and mighty-armed son of Pritha, more afflicted than his uncle, with eyes bathed in tears, touched his uncle's feet, O Bharata. The mighty-armed Anakadundubhi wished to smell the head of his sister's son but failed to do it, O slayer of foes. The old man of mighty arms, deeply afflicted, embraced Partha with his arms and wept aloud, remembering his sons, brothers, grandsons, daughters' sons, and friends.

"'Vasudeva said, "Without beholding those heroes, O Arjuna, who had subjugated all the kings of the Earth and the Daityas a hundred times, I am still alive! Methinks, I have no death! Through the fault of those two heroes who were thy dear disciples and who were much regarded by thee, also, O Partha, the Vrishnis have been destroyed. Those two who were regarded as Atirathas amongst the foremost of the Vrishnis, and referring to whom in course of conversation thou wert wont to indulge in pride, and who, O chief of Kuru's race, were ever dear to Krishna himself, alas, those two, O Dhananjaya, have been the chief causes of the destruction of the Vrishnis! I do not censure the son of Sini or the son of Hridika, O Arjuna. I do not censure Akrura or the son of Rukmini. No doubt, the curse (of the Rishis) is the sole cause. How is it that that lord of the universe, the slayer of Madhu, who had put forth his prowess for achieving the destruction of Kesin and Kansa, and Chaidya swelling with pride, and Ekalavya, the son of the ruler of the Nishadas, and the Kalingas and the Magadhas, and the Gandharas and the king of Kasi, and many rulers assembled together in the midst of the desert, many heroes belonging to the East and the South, and many kings of the mountainous regions, alas, how could he remain indifferent to such a calamity as the curse denounced by the Rishis? Thyself, Narada, and the Munis, knew him to be the eternal and sinless Govinda, the Deity of unfading glory. Alas, being puissant Vishnu himself, he witnessed, without interfering, the destruction of his kinsmen! My son must have himself allowed all this to happen. He was the Lord of the universe. He did not, however, wish to falsify the words of Gandhari and the Rishis, O scorcher of foes. In thy very sight, O hero, thy grandson, who had been slain by Ashvatthama, was revived through his energy. That friend, however, of yours did not wish to protect his kinsmen. Beholding his sons and grandsons and brothers and friends lying dead, he said unto me these words, O chief of Bharata's race, 'The destruction of this our race has at last come. Vibhatsu will come to this city, Dwaravati. Tell him what has occurred, this great carnage of the Vrishnis. I have no doubt that as soon as he will hear of the destruction of the Yadus, that hero of mighty energy will come here without any loss of time. Know, O father, that I am Arjuna and Arjuna is myself. That should be done by thee which he would say. The son of Pandu will do what is best for the women and the children. Even he will perform thy funeral rites. This city of Dwaravati, after Arjuna's departure, will, with its walls and edifices, be swallowed up by the ocean without any delay. As regards myself, retiring to some sacred place, I shall bide my hour, with the intelligent Rama in my company, observing strict vows all the while.' Having said these words unto me, Hrishikesa of inconceivable prowess, leaving me with the children, has gone away to some spot which I do not know. Thinking of those two high-souled brothers of thine, as also of the terrible carnage of my kinsmen, I have abstained from all food, and am emaciated with grief. I shall neither eat, nor live. By good luck thou meetest me, O son of Pandu. Do thou accomplish all, O Partha, that Krishna has said. This kingdom, with all these women, and all the wealth here, is thine now, O son of Pritha. As regards myself, O slayer of foes, I shall cast off my life-breaths dear though they be."'"

7

"Vaishampayana said: 'That scorcher of foes, Vibhatsu, thus addressed by his maternal uncle, replied, with great cheerlessness of heart, unto Vasudeva who was equally cheerless, saying, "O uncle, I am unable to look at this Earth when she is reft of that hero of Vrishni's race and those my other kinsmen. The king and Bhimasena and Sahadeva and Nakula and Yajnaseni, numbering the sixth, are of the same mind with myself in this matter. The time has come for the departure of the king also. Know this, that the hour of our departure too is at hand. Thou art the foremost of those that are well conversant with the course of time. I shall, however, O chastiser of foes, first remove to Indraprastha the women of the Vrishni race as also the children and the aged." Having said so unto his uncle, Arjuna next addressed Daruka, saying, "I wish to see without any delay the chief officers of the Vrishni heroes." Having uttered these words, the heroic Arjuna, grieving for those great car-warriors (who had been slain), entered the great hall of the Yadavas (where they used to hold their court), called Sudharma. When he had taken his seat there, all the citizens, including the Brahmanas, and all the ministers of state came and stood surrounding him. Then Partha, more grieved than they, addressed those grieving and cheerless citizens and officers who were more dead than alive, and said these words that were well suited to the occasion: "I shall take away with me the remnants of the Vrishnis and the Andhakas. The sea will soon engulf this city. Equip all your cars and place on them all your wealth. This Vajra (the grandson of Krishna) will be your king at Shakraprastha. On the seventh day from this, at sunrise, we shall set out. Make your preparations without delay."

"'Thus addressed by Pritha's son of pure deeds, all of them hastened their preparations with eagerness for achieving their safety. Arjuna passed that night in the mansion of Keshava. He was suddenly overwhelmed with great grief and stupefaction. When morning dawned, Vasudeva of great energy and prowess attained, through the aid of Yoga, to the highest goal. A loud and heart-rending sound of wailing was heard in Vasudeva's mansion, uttered by the weeping ladies. They were seen with dishevelled hair and divested of ornaments and floral wreaths. Beating their breasts with their hands, they indulged in heart-rending lamentations. Those foremost of women, Devaki and Bhadra and Rohini and Madira threw themselves on the bodies of their lord. Then Partha caused the body of his uncle to be carried out on a costly vehicle borne on the shoulders of men. It was followed by all the citizens of Dwaraka and the people of the provinces, all of whom, deeply afflicted by grief, had been well-affected towards the deceased hero. Before that vehicle were borne the umbrella which had been held over his head at the conclusion of the horse-sacrifice he had achieved while living, and also the blazing fires he had daily worshipped, with the priests that had used to attend to them. The body of the hero was followed by his wives decked in ornaments and surrounded by thousands of women and thousands of their daughters-in-law. The last rites were then performed at that spot which had been agreeable to him while he was alive. The four wives of that heroic son of Sura ascended the funeral pyre and were consumed with the body of their lord. All of them attained to those regions of felicity which were his. The son of Pandu burnt the body of his uncle together with those four wives of his, using diverse kinds of scents and perfumed wood. As the funeral pyre blazed up, a loud sound was heard of the burning wood and other combustible materials, along with the clear chant of Samans and the wailing of the citizens and others who witnessed the rite. After it was all over, the boys of the Vrishni and Andhaka races, headed by Vajra, as also the ladies, offered oblations of water to the high-souled hero.

"'Phalguna, who was careful in observing every duty, having caused this duty to be performed, proceeded, O chief of Bharata's race, next to the place where the Vrishnis were slaughtered. The Kuru prince, beholding them lying slaughtered all around, became exceedingly cheerless. He, however, did what was required to be done in view of that which had happened. The last rites were performed, according to the order of seniority, unto the bodies of those heroes slain by the iron bolts born, by virtue of the curse denounced by the Brahmanas, of the blades of Eraka grass. Searching out the bodies then of Rama and Vasudeva, Arjuna caused them to be burnt by persons skilled in that act. The son of Pandu, having next performed duly those sraddha rites that are done to the dead, quickly set out on the seventh day, mounting on his car. The widows of the Vrishni heroes, wailing aloud, followed the high-souled son of Pandu, Dhananjaya, on cars drawn by bullocks and mules and camels. All were in deep affliction. The servants of the Vrishnis, their horsemen, and their car-warriors too, followed the procession. The citizens and the inhabitants of the country, at the command of Pritha's son, set out at the same time and proceeded, surrounding that cavalcade destitute of heroes and numbering only women and the aged and the children. The warriors who fought from the backs of elephants proceeded on elephants as huge as hills. The foot-soldiers also set out, together with the reserves. The children of the Andhaka and the Vrishni races, all followed Arjuna. The Brahmanas and Kshatriyas, and Vaisyas, and wealthy Sudras, set out, keeping before them the 16,000 women that had formed Vasudeva's harem, and Vajra, the grandson of the intelligent Krishna. The widows of the other heroes of the Bhoja, the Vrishni, and the Andhaka races, lordless now, that set out with Arjuna, numbered many millions. That foremost of car-warriors, that conqueror of hostile towns, the son of Pritha, escorted this vast procession of Vrishnis, which still abounded with wealth, and which looked like a veritable ocean.

"'After all the people had set out, the ocean, that home of sharks and alligators, flooded Dwaraka, which still teemed with wealth of every kind, with its waters. Whatever portion of the ground was passed over, ocean immediately flooded over with his waters. Beholding this wonderful sight, the inhabitants of Dwaraka walked faster and faster, saying, "Wonderful is the course of fate!" Dhananjaya, after abandoning Dwaraka, proceeded by slow marches, causing the Vrishni women to rest in pleasant forests and mountains and by the sides of delightful streams. Arrived at the country of the five waters, the puissant Dhananjaya planted a rich encampment in the midst of a land that abounded with corn and kine and other animals. Beholding those lordless widows escorted by Pritha's son alone O Bharata, the robbers felt a great temptation (for plunder). Then those sinful wretches, with hearts overwhelmed by cupidity, those Abhiras of ill omen, assembled together and held a consultation. They said, "Here there is only one bowman, Arjuna. The cavalcade consists of children and the old. He escorts them, transgressing us. The warriors (of the Vrishnis) are without energy." Then those robbers, numbering by thousands, and armed with clubs, rushed towards the procession of the Vrishnis, desirous of plunder. Urged by the perverse course of time they fell upon that vast concourse, frightening it with loud leonine shouts and desirous of slaughter. The son of Kunti, suddenly ceasing to advance along the path, turned, with his followers, towards the place where the robbers had attacked the procession. Smiling the while, that mighty-armed warrior addressed the assailants, saying, "You sinful wretches, forbear, if ye love your lives. Ye will rue this when I pierce your bodies with my shafts and take your lives." Though thus addressed by that hero, they disregarded his words, and though repeatedly dissuaded, they fell upon Arjuna. Then Arjuna endeavoured to string his large, indestructible, celestial bow with some effort. He succeeded with great difficulty in stringing it, when the battle had become furious. He then began to think of his celestial weapons but they would not come to his mind. Beholding that furious battle, the loss of the might of his arm, and the non-appearance of his celestial weapons, Arjuna became greatly ashamed. The Vrishni warriors including the foot-soldiers, the elephant-warriors, and the car-men, failed to rescue those Vrishni women that were being snatched away by the robbers. The concourse was very large. The robbers assailed it at different points. Arjuna tried his best to protect it, but could not succeed. In the very sight of all the warriors, many foremost of ladies were dragged away, while others went away with the robbers of their own accord. The puissant Arjuna, supported by the servants of the Vrishnis, struck the robbers with shafts sped from Gandiva. Soon, however, O king, his shafts were exhausted. In former days his shafts had been inexhaustible. Now, however, they proved otherwise. Finding his shafts exhausted, he became deeply afflicted with grief. The son of Indra then began to strike the robbers with the horns of his bow. Those Mlecchas, however, O Janamejaya, in the very sight of Partha, retreated, taking away with them many foremost ladies of the Vrishnis and Andhakas. The puissant Dhananjaya regarded it all as the work of destiny. Filled with sorrow he breathed heavy sighs at the thought of the non-appearance of his (celestial) weapons, the loss of the might of his arms, the refusal of his bow to obey him, and the exhaustion of his shafts. Regarding it all as the work of destiny, he became exceedingly cheerless. He then ceased, O king, to make further efforts, saying, he had not the power which he had before. The high-souled one, taking with him the remnant of the Vrishni women, and the wealth that was still with them, reached Kurukshetra. Thus bringing with him the remnant of the Vrishnis, he established them at different places. He established the son of Kritavarma at the city called Marttikavat, with the remnant of the women of the Bhoja king. Escorting the remainder, with children and old men and women, the son of Pandu established them, who were reft of heroes, in the city of Indraprastha. The dear son of Yuyudhana, with a company of old men and children and women, the righteous-souled Arjuna established on the banks of the Sarasvati. The rule of Indraprastha was given to Vajra. The widows of Akrura then desired to retire into the woods. Vajra asked them repeatedly to desist, but they did not listen to him. Rukmini, the princess of Gandhara, Saivya, Haimavati, and queen Jamvabati ascended the funeral pyre. Satyabhama and other dear wives of Krishna entered the woods, O king, resolved to set themselves to the practice of penances. They began to live on fruits and roots and pass their time in the contemplation of Hari. Going beyond the Himavat, they took up their abode in a place called Kalpa. Those men who had followed Arjuna from Dwaravati, were distributed into groups, and bestowed upon Vajra. Having done all these acts suited to the occasion, Arjuna, with eyes bathed in tears, then entered the retreat of Vyasa. There he beheld the Island-born Rishi seated at his ease.'"

8

"Vaishampayana said: 'As Arjuna entered the asylum of the truthful Rishi, he beheld the son of Satyavati seated in a secluded spot.

"'Approaching that Rishi of high vows and endued with a knowledge of all duties, he said, "I am Arjuna," and then awaited his pleasure. Satyavati's son, endued with high penances, answered, saying "Welcome!" Of tranquil soul, the great Muni further said, "Take thy seat." Seeing that the son of Pritha was exceedingly cheerless and breathing heavy sighs repeatedly and filled with despair, Vyasa addressed him, saying, "Hast thou been sprinkled with water from anybody's nails or hair, or the end of anybody's cloth, or from the mouth of a jar? Hast thou had sexual congress with any woman before the cessation of her functional flow? Hast thou slain a Brahmana? Hast thou been vanquished in battle? Thou lookest like one shorn of prosperity. I do not know that thou hast been defeated by anyone. Why then, O chief of Bharata's race, this exceedingly dejected aspect? It behoveth thee, O son of Pritha, to tell me all, if, indeed, there be no harm in telling it."

"'Arjuna said, "He whose complexion was like that of a (newly-risen) cloud, he whose eyes were like a pair of large lotus petals, Krishna, has, with Rama, cast off his body and ascended to Heaven. At Prabhasa, through iron bolts generated by the curse denounced by Brahmanas, the destruction has taken place of the Vrishni heroes. Awful hath that carnage been, and not even a single hero has escaped. The heroes of the Bhoja, the Andhaka, and the Vrishni races, O Brahmana, who were all endued with high souls, great might, and leonine pride, have slaughtered one another in battle. Possessed of arms that looked like maces of iron, and capable of bearing the strokes of heavy clubs and darts, alas, they have all been slain with blades of Eraka grass. Behold the perverse course of Time. 500,000 mighty-armed warriors have thus been laid low. Encountering one another, they have met with destruction. Thinking repeatedly of this carnage of the Yadava warriors of immeasurable energy and of the illustrious Krishna, I fail to derive peace of mind. The death of the wielder of Sarnga is as incredible as the drying up of the ocean, the displacement of a mountain, the falling down of the vault of heaven, or the cooling property of fire. Deprived of the company of the Vrishni heroes, I desire not to live in this world. Another incident has happened that is more painful than this, O thou that art possessed of wealth of penances. Repeatedly thinking of it, my heart is breaking. In my very sight, O Brahmana, thousands of Vrishni ladies were carried away by the Abhiras of the country of the five waters, who assailed us. Taking up my bow I found myself unequal to even string it. The might that had existed in my arms seemed to have disappeared on that occasion. O great ascetic, my weapons of diverse kinds failed to make their appearance. Soon, again, my shafts became exhausted. That person of immeasurable soul, of four arms, wielding the conch, the discus, and the mace, clad in yellow robes, dark of complexion, and possessing eyes resembling lotus-petals, is no longer seen by me. Alas, reft of Govinda, what have I to live for, dragging my life in sorrow? He who used to stalk in advance of my car, that divine form endued with great splendour and unfading puissance, consuming as he proceeded all hostile warriors, can no longer be seen by me. No longer beholding him who by his energy first burnt all hostile troops whom I afterwards despatched with shafts sped from Gandiva, I am filled with grief and my head swims, O best of men. Penetrated with cheerlessness and despair, I fail to obtain peace of mind. I dare not live, reft of the heroic Janardana. As soon as I heard that Vishnu had left the Earth, my eyes became dim and all things disappeared from my vision. O best of men, it behoveth thee to tell me what is good for me now, for I am now a wanderer with an empty heart, despoiled of my kinsmen and of my possession."

"'Vyasa said, "The mighty car-warriors of the Vrishni and the Andhaka races have all been consumed by the Brahmana's curse. O chief of Kuru's race, it behoveth thee not to grieve for their destruction. That which has happened had been ordained. It was the destiny of those high-souled warriors. Krishna suffered it to take place although he was fully competent to baffle it. Govinda was able to alter the very course of the universe with all its mobile and immobile creatures. What need then be said of the curse of even high-souled Brahmanas? He who used to proceed in front of thy car, armed with discus and mace, through affection for thee, was the four-armed Vasudeva, that ancient rishi. That high-souled one of expansive eyes, Krishna, having lightened the burthen of the Earth and cast off his (human) body, has attained to his own high seat. By thee also, O foremost of men, with Bhima for thy helpmate and the twins, O mighty-armed hero, has the great work of the gods been accomplished. O foremost one of Kuru's race, I regard thee and thy brothers as crowned with success, for ye have accomplished the great purpose of your lives. The time has come for your departure from the world. Even this, O puissant one, is what is beneficial for you now. Even thus, understanding and prowess and foresight, O Bharata, arise when days of prosperity have not outrun. These very acquisitions disappear when the hour of adversity comes. All this has Time for its root. Time is, indeed, the seed of the universe, O Dhananjaya. It is Time, again, that withdraws everything at its pleasure. One becomes mighty, and, again, losing that might, becomes weak. One becomes a master and rules others, and, again, losing that position, becomes a servant for obeying the behests of others. Thy weapons, having achieved success, have gone away to the place they came from. They will, again, come into thy hands when the Time for their coming approaches. The time has come, O Bharata, for you all to attain to the highest goal. Even this is what I regard to be highly beneficial for you all, O chief of Bharata's race."

"Vaishampayana continued: 'Having heard these words of Vyasa of immeasurable energy, the son of Pritha, receiving his permission, returned to the city named after the elephant. Entering it, the hero approached Yudhishthira and informed him of all that had taken place with reference to the Vrishnis.'"

The end of Mausala-parva.

BOOK 17
Mahaprasthanika-parva

1

Om! Having bowed down unto Narayana, and to Nara, the foremost of men, as also to the goddess Sarasvati, should the word "Jaya" be uttered.

"Janamejaya said: 'Having heard of that encounter with iron bolts between the heroes of the Vrishni and the Andhaka races, and having been informed also of Krishna's ascension to Heaven, what did the Pandavas do?'

"Vaishampayana said: 'Having heard the particulars of the great slaughter of the Vrishnis, the Kaurava king set his heart on leaving the world. He addressed Arjuna, saying, O thou of great intelligence, it is Time that cooks every creature (in his cauldron). I think that what has happened is due to the cords of Time (with which he binds us all). It behoveth thee also to see it.

"'Thus addressed by his brother, the son of Kunti only repeated the word "Time, Time!" and fully endorsed the view of his eldest brother gifted with great intelligence. Ascertaining the resolution of Arjuna, Bhimasena and the twins fully endorsed the words that Arjuna had said. Resolved to retire from the world for earning merit, they brought Yuyutsu before them. Yudhishthira made over the kingdom to the son of his uncle by his Vaisya wife. Installing Parikshit also on their throne, as king, the eldest brother of the Pandavas, filled with sorrow, addressed Subhadra, saying, This son of thy son will be the king of the Kurus. The survivor of the Yadus, Vajra, has been made a king. Parikshit will rule in Hastinapura, while the Yadava prince, Vajra, will rule in Shakraprastha. He should be protected by thee. Never set thy heart on unrighteousness.

"'Having said these words, king Yudhishthira the just, along with his brothers, promptly offered oblations of water unto Vasudeva of great intelligence, as also unto his old maternal uncle and Rama and others. He then duly performed the Sraddhas of all those deceased kinsmen of his. The king, in honour of Hari and naming him repeatedly, fed the Island-born Vyasa, and Narada, and Markandeya possessed of wealth of penances, and

Yajnavalkya of Bharadwaja's race, with many delicious viands. In honour of Krishna, he also gave away many jewels and gems, and robes and clothes, and villages, and horses and cars, and female slaves by hundreds and thousands unto foremost of Brahmanas. Summoning the citizens, Kripa was installed as the preceptor and Parikshit was made over to him as his disciple, O chief of Bharata's race.

"'Then Yudhishthira once more summoned all his subjects. The royal sage informed them of his intentions. The citizens and the inhabitants of the provinces, hearing the king's words, became filled with anxiety and disapproved of them. "This should never be done," said they unto the king. The monarch, well versed with the changes brought about by time, did not listen to their counsels. Possessed of righteous soul, he persuaded the people to sanction his views. He then set his heart on leaving the world. His brothers also formed the same resolution. Then Dharma's son, Yudhishthira, the king of the Kurus, casting off his ornaments, wore barks of trees. Bhima and Arjuna and the twins, and Draupadi also of great fame, similarly clad themselves in bark of trees, O king. Having caused the preliminary rites of religion, O chief of Bharata's race, which were to bless them in the accomplishment of their design, those foremost of men cast off their sacred fires into the water. The ladies, beholding the princes in that guise, wept aloud. They seemed to look as they had looked in days before, when with Draupadi forming the sixth in number they set out from the capital after their defeat at dice. The brothers, however, were all very cheerful at the prospect of retirement. Ascertaining the intentions of Yudhishthira and seeing the destruction of the Vrishnis, no other course of action could please them then.

"'The five brothers, with Draupadi forming the sixth, and a dog forming the seventh, set out on their journey. Indeed, even thus did king Yudhishthira depart, himself the head of a party of seven, from the city named after the elephant. The citizens and the ladies of the royal household followed them for some distance. None of them, however, could venture to address the king for persuading him to give up his intention. The denizens of the city then returned; Kripa and others stood around Yuyutsu as their centre. Ulupi, the daughter of the Naga chief, O thou of Kunti's race, entered the waters of Ganga. The princess Chitrangada set out for the capital of Manipura. The other ladies who were the grandmothers of Parikshit centered around him. Meanwhile the high-souled Pandavas, O thou of Kuru's race, and Draupadi of great fame, having observed the preliminary fast, set out with their faces towards the east. Setting themselves on Yoga, those high-souled ones, resolved to observe the religion of Renunciation, traversed through various countries and reached diverse rivers and seas. Yudhishthira, proceeded first. Behind him was Bhima; next walked Arjuna; after him were the twins in the order of their birth; behind them all, O foremost one of Bharata's race, proceeded Draupadi, that first of women, possessed of great beauty, of dark complexion, and endued with eyes resembling lotus petals. While the Pandavas set out for the forest, a dog followed them.

"'Proceeding on, those heroes reached the sea of red waters. Dhananjaya had not cast off his celestial bow Gandiva, nor his couple of inexhaustible quivers, actuated, O king, by the cupidity that attaches one to things of great value. The Pandavas there beheld the deity of fire standing before them like a hill. Closing their way, the god stood there in his embodied form. The deity of seven flames then addressed the Pandavas, saying, "Ye heroic sons of Pandu, know me for the deity of fire. O mighty-armed Yudhishthira, O Bhimasena that art a scorcher of foes, O Arjuna, and ye twins of great courage, listen to what I say! Ye foremost ones of Kuru's race, I am the god of fire. The forest of Khandava was burnt by me, through the puissance of Arjuna and of Narayana himself. Let your brother Phalguna proceed to the woods after casting off Gandiva, that high weapon. He has no longer any need of it. That precious discus, which was with the high-souled Krishna, has disappeared (from the world). When the time again comes, it will come back into his hands. This foremost of bows, Gandiva, was procured by me from Varuna for the use of Partha. Let it be made over to Varuna himself."

"'At this, all the brothers urged Dhananjaya to do what the deity said. He then threw into the waters (of the sea) both the bow and the couple of inexhaustible quivers. After this, O chief of Bharata's race, the god of the fire disappeared then and there. The heroic sons of Pandu next proceeded with their faces turned towards the south. Then, by the northern coast of the salt sea, those princes of Bharata's race proceeded to the south-west. Turning next towards the west, they beheld the city of Dwaraka covered by the ocean. Turning next to the north, those foremost ones proceeded on. Observant of Yoga, they were desirous of making a round of the whole Earth.'"

2

"Vaishampayana said: 'Those princes of restrained souls and devoted to Yoga, proceeding to the north, beheld Himavat, that very large mountain. Crossing the Himavat, they beheld a vast desert of sand. They then saw the mighty mountain Meru, the foremost of all high-peaked mountains. As those mighty ones were proceeding quickly, all rapt in Yoga, Yajnaseni, falling of from Yoga, dropped down on the Earth. Beholding her fallen down, Bhimasena of great strength addressed king Yudhishthira the just, saying, "O scorcher of foes, this princess never did any sinful act. Tell us what the cause is for which Krishna has fallen down on the Earth!"

"'Yudhishthira said: "O best of men, though we were all equal unto her she had great partiality for Dhananjaya. She obtains the fruit of that conduct today, O best of men."'

"Vaishampayana continued: 'Having said this, that foremost one of Bharata's race proceeded on. Of righteous soul, that foremost of men, endued with great intelligence, went on, with mind intent on itself. Then Sahadeva of great learning fell down on the Earth. Beholding him drop down, Bhima addressed the king, saying, "He who with great humility used to serve us all, alas, why is that son of Madravati fallen down on the Earth?"

"'Yudhishthira said, "He never thought anybody his equal in wisdom. It is for that fault that this prince has fallen down."

"Vaishampayana continued: 'Having said this, the king proceeded, leaving Sahadeva there. Indeed, Kunti's son Yudhishthira went on, with his brothers and with the dog. Beholding both Krishna and the Pandava Sahadeva fallen down, the brave Nakula, whose love for kinsmen was very great, fell down himself. Upon the falling down of the heroic Nakula of great personal beauty, Bhima once more addressed the king, saying, "This brother of ours who was endued with righteousness without incompleteness, and who always obeyed our behests, this Nakula who was unrivalled for beauty, has fallen down."

"'Thus addressed by Bhimasena, Yudhishthira said, with respect to Nakula, these words: "He was of righteous soul and the foremost of all persons endued with intelligence. He, however, thought that there was nobody that equalled him in beauty of person. Indeed, he regarded himself as superior to all in that respect. It is for this that Nakula has fallen down. Know this, O Vrikodara. What has been ordained for a person, O hero, must have to be endured by him."

"'Beholding Nakula and the others fall down, Pandu's son Arjuna of white steeds, that slayer of hostile heroes, fell down in great grief of heart. When that foremost of men, who was endued with the energy of Shakra, had fallen down, indeed, when that invincible hero was on the point of death, Bhima said unto the king, "I do not recollect any untruth uttered by this high-souled one. Indeed, not even in jest did he say anything false. What then is that for whose evil consequence this one has fallen down on the Earth?"

"'Yudhishthira said, "Arjuna had said that he would consume all our foes in a single day. Proud of his heroism, he did not, however, accomplish what he had said. Hence has he fallen down. This Phalguna disregarded all wielders of bows. One desirous of prosperity should never indulge in such sentiments."'

"Vaishampayana continued: 'Having said so, the king proceeded on. Then Bhima fell down. Having fallen down, Bhima addressed king Yudhishthira the just, saying, "O king, behold, I who am thy darling have fallen down. For what reason have I dropped down? Tell me if thou knowest it."

"'Yudhishthira said, "Thou wert a great eater, and thou didst use to boast of thy strength. Thou never didst attend, O Bhima, to the wants of others while eating. It is for that, O Bhima, that thou hast fallen down."

"'Having said these words, the mighty-armed Yudhishthira proceeded on, without looking back. He had only one companion, the dog of which I have repeatedly spoken to thee, that followed him now.'"

3

"Vaishampayana said: 'Then Shakra, causing the firmament and the Earth to be filled by a loud sound, came to the son of Pritha on a car and asked him to ascend it. Beholding his brothers fallen on the Earth, king Yudhishthira the just said unto that deity of a 1,000 eyes these words: "My brothers have all dropped down here. They must go with me. Without them by me I do not wish to go to Heaven, O lord of all the deities. The delicate princess (Draupadi) deserving of every comfort, O Purandara, should go with us. It behoveth thee to permit this."

"'Shakra said, "Thou shalt behold thy brothers in Heaven. They have reached it before thee. Indeed, thou shalt see all of them there, with Krishna. Do not yield to grief, O chief of the Bharatas. Having cast off their human bodies they have gone there, O chief of Bharata's race. As regards thee, it is ordained that thou shalt go thither in this very body of thine."

"'Yudhishthira said, "This dog, O lord of the Past and the Present, is exceedingly devoted to me. He should go with me. My heart is full of compassion for him."

"'Shakra said, "Immortality and a condition equal to mine, O king, prosperity extending in all directions, and high success, and all the felicities of Heaven, thou hast won today. Do thou cast off this dog. In this there will be no cruelty."

"'Yudhishthira said, "O thou of a 1,000 eyes. O thou that art of righteous behaviour, it is exceedingly difficult for one that is of righteous behaviour to perpetrate an act that is unrighteous. I do not desire that union with prosperity for which I shall have to cast off one that is devoted to me."

"'Indra said, "There is no place in Heaven for persons with dogs. Besides, the (deities called) Krodhavasas take away all the merits of such persons. Reflecting on this, act, O king Yudhishthira the just. Do thou abandon this dog. There is no cruelty in this."

"'Yudhishthira said, "It has been said that the abandonment of one that is devoted is infinitely sinful. It is equal to the sin that one incurs by slaying a Brahmana. Hence, O great Indra, I shall not abandon this dog today from desire of my happiness. Even this is my vow steadily pursued, that I never give up a person that is terrified, nor one that is devoted to me, nor one that seeks my protection, saying that he is destitute, nor one that is afflicted, nor one that has come to me, nor one that is weak in protecting oneself, nor one that is solicitous of life. I shall never give up such a one till my own life is at an end."

"'Indra said, "Whatever gifts, or sacrifices spread out, or libations poured on the sacred fire, are seen by a dog, are taken away by the Krodhavasas. Do thou, therefore, abandon this dog. By abandoning this dog thou wilt attain to the region of the deities. Having abandoned thy brothers and Krishna, thou hast, O hero, acquired a region of felicity by thy own deeds. Why art thou so stupefied? Thou hast renounced everything. Why then dost thou not renounce this dog?" Yudhishthira said, "This is well known in all the worlds that there is neither friendship nor enmity with those that are dead. When my brothers and Krishna died, I was unable to revive them. Hence it was that I abandoned them. I did not, however, abandon them as long as they were alive. To frighten one that has sought protection, the slaying of a woman, the theft of what belongs to a Brahmana, and injuring a friend, each of these four, O Shakra, is I think equal to the abandonment of one that is devoted."'

"Vaishampayana continued: 'Hearing these words of king Yudhishthira the just, (the dog became transformed into) the deity of Righteousness, who, well pleased, said these words unto him in a sweet voice fraught with praise.

"'Dharma said: "Thou art well born, O king of kings, and possessed of the intelligence and the good conduct of Pandu. Thou hast compassion for all creatures, O Bharata, of which this is a bright example. Formerly, O son, thou wert once examined by me in the woods of Dwaita, where thy brothers of great prowess met with (an appearance of) death. Disregarding both thy brothers Bhima and Arjuna, thou didst wish for the revival of Nakula from thy desire of doing good to thy (step-) mother. On the present occasion, thinking the dog to be devoted to thee, thou hast renounced the very car of the celestials instead of renouncing him. Hence, O king, there is no one in Heaven that is equal to thee. Hence, O Bharata, regions of inexhaustible felicity are thine. Thou hast won them, O chief of the Bharatas, and thine is a celestial and high goal."'

"Vaishampayana continued: 'Then Dharma, and Shakra, and the Maruts, and the Ashvinis, and other deities, and the celestial Rishis, causing Yudhishthira to ascend on a car, proceeded to Heaven. Those beings crowned with success and capable of going everywhere at will, rode their respective cars. King Yudhishthira, that perpetuator of Kuru's race, riding on that car, ascended quickly, causing the entire welkin to blaze with his effulgence. Then Narada, that foremost of all speakers, endued with penances, and conversant with all the worlds, from amidst that concourse of deities, said these words: "All those royal sages that are here have their achievements transcended by those of Yudhishthira. Covering all the worlds by his fame and splendour and by his wealth of conduct, he has attained to Heaven in his own (human) body. None else than the son of Pandu has been heard to achieve this."

"'Hearing these words of Narada, the righteous-souled king, saluting the deities and all the royal sages there present, said, "Happy or miserable, whatever the region be that is now my brothers', I desire to proceed to. I do not wish to go anywhere else."

"'Hearing this speech of the king, the chief of the deities, Purandara, said these words fraught with noble sense: "Do thou live in this place, O king of kings, which thou hast won by thy meritorious deeds. Why dost thou still cherish human affections? Thou hast attained to great success, the like of which no other man has ever been able to attain. Thy brothers, O delighter of the Kurus, have succeeded in winning regions of felicity. Human affections still touch thee. This is Heaven. Behold these celestial Rishis and Siddhas who have attained to the region of the gods."

"'Gifted with great intelligence, Yudhishthira answered the chief of the deities once more, saying, "O conqueror of Daityas, I venture not to dwell anywhere separated from them. I desire to go there, where my brothers have gone. I wish to go there where that foremost of women, Draupadi, of ample proportions and darkish complexion and endued with great intelligence and righteous of conduct, has gone."'"

The end of Mahaprasthanika-parva.

BOOK 18
Svargarohanika-parva

1

Om! Having bowed down into Narayana, and to Nara, the foremost of men, as also to the goddess Sarasvati, should the word "Jaya" be uttered.

"Janamejaya said, 'Having attained to Heaven, what regions were respectively attained by my grandsires of old, viz., the Pandavas and the sons of Dhritarashtra? I desire to hear this. I think that thou art conversant with everything, having been taught by the great Rishi Vyasa of wonderful feats.'

"Vaishampayana said, 'Listen now to what thy grandsires, Yudhishthira and others, did after having attained to Heaven, that place of the deities. Arrived at Heaven, king Yudhishthira the just, beheld Duryodhana endued with prosperity and seated on an excellent seat. He blazed with effulgence like the sun and wore all those signs of glory which belong to heroes. And he was in the company of many deities of blazing effulgence and of Sadhyas of righteous deeds. Yudhishthira, beholding Duryodhana and his prosperity, became suddenly filled with rage and turned back from the sight.

"'He loudly addressed his companions, saying, "I do not desire to share regions of felicity with Duryodhana who was stained by cupidity and possessed of little foresight. It was for him that friends, and kinsmen, over the whole Earth were slaughtered by us whom he had afflicted greatly in the deep forest. It was for him that the virtuous princess of Panchala, Draupadi of faultless features, our wife, was dragged into the midst of the assembly before all our seniors. Ye gods, I have no desire to even behold Suyodhana. I wish to go there where my brothers are."

"'Narada, smiling, told him, "It should not be so, O king of kings. While residing in Heaven, all enmities cease. O mighty-armed Yudhishthira, do not say so about king Duryodhana. Hear my words. Here is king Duryodhana. He is worshipped with the gods by those righteous men and those foremost of kings who are now denizens of Heaven. By causing his body to be poured as a libation on the fire of battle, he has obtained the end that consists in attainment of the region for heroes. You and your brothers, who were veritable gods on Earth, were always persecuted by this one. Yet through his observance of Kshatriya practices he has attained to this region. This lord of Earth was not terrified in a situation fraught with terror.

"'"O son, thou shouldst not bear in mind the woes inflicted on thee on account of the match at dice. It behoveth thee not to remember the afflictions of Draupadi. It behoveth thee not to remember the other woes which were yours in consequence of the acts of your kinsmen, the woes, viz., that were due to battle or to other situations. Do thou meet Duryodhana now according to the ordinances of polite intercourse. This is Heaven, O lord of men. There can be no enmities here."

"'Though thus addressed by Narada, the Kuru king Yudhishthira, endued with great intelligence, enquired about his brothers and said, "If these eternal regions reserved for heroes be Duryodhana's, that unrighteous and sinful wight, that man who was the destroyer of friends and of the whole world, that man for whose sake the entire Earth was devastated with all her horses and elephants and human beings, that wight for whose sake we were burnt with wrath in thinking of how best we might remedy our wrongs, I desire to see what regions have been attained by those high-souled heroes, my brothers of high vows, steady achievers of promises, truthful in speech, and distinguished for courage. The high-souled Karna, the son of Kunti, incapable of being baffled in battle, Dhrishtadyumna, Satyaki, the sons of Dhrishtadyumna and those other Kshatriyas who met with death in the observance of Kshatriya practices, where are those lords of Earth, O Brahmana? I do not see them here, O Narada. I desire to see, O Narada, Virata and Drupada and the other great Kshatriyas headed by Dhrishtaketu, as also Shikhandi, the Panchala prince, the sons of Draupadi, and Abhimanyu, irresistible in battle."'"

2

"'Yudhishthira said, "Ye deities, I do not see here Radha's son of immeasurable prowess, as also my high-souled brothers, and Yudhamanyu and Uttamaujas, those great car-warriors that poured their bodies (as libations) on the fire of battle, those kings and princes that met with death for my sake in battle. Where are those great car-warriors that possessed the prowess of tigers? Have those foremost of men acquired this region? If those great car-warriors have obtained these regions, then only do you know, ye gods, that I shall reside here with those high-souled ones. If this auspicious and eternal region has not been acquired by those kings, then know, ye gods, that without those brothers and kinsmen of mine, I shall not live here. At the time of performing the water rites (after the battle), I heard my mother say, 'Do thou offer oblations of water unto Karna.' Since hearing those words of my mother, I am burning with grief. I grieve also incessantly at this, ye gods, that when I marked the resemblance between the feet of my mother and those of Karna of immeasurable soul, I did not immediately place myself under orders of that afflicter of hostile ranks. Ourselves joined with Karna, Shakra himself would have been unable to vanquish in battle. Wherever may that child of Surya be, I desire to see him. Alas, his relationship with us being unknown, I caused him to be slain by Arjuna. Bhima also of terrible prowess and dearer to me than my life-breaths, Arjuna too, resembling Indra himself, the twins also that resembled the Destroyer himself in prowess, I desire to behold. I wish to see the princess of Panchala, whose conduct was always righteous. I wish not to stay here. I tell you the truth. Ye foremost ones among the deities, what is Heaven to me if I am dissociated from my brothers? That is Heaven where those brothers of mine are. This, in my opinion, is not Heaven."

"'The gods said, "If thou longest to be there, go then, O son, without delay. At the command of the chief of the deities, we are ready to do what is agreeable to thee."'

"Vaishampayana continued: 'Having said so, the gods then ordered the celestial messenger, O scorcher of foes, saying, "Do thou show unto Yudhishthira his friends and kinsmen." Then the royal son of Kunti and the celestial messenger proceeded together, O foremost of kings, to that place where those chiefs of men (whom Yudhishthira had wished to see) were. The celestial messenger proceeded first, the king followed him behind. The path was inauspicious and difficult and trodden by men of sinful deeds. It was enveloped in thick darkness, and covered with hair and moss forming its grassy vesture. Polluted with the stench of sinners, and miry with flesh and blood, it abounded with gadflies and stinging bees and gnats and was endangered by the inroads of grisly bears. Rotting corpses lay here and there. Overspread with bones and hair, it was noisome with worms and insects. It was skirted all along with a blazing fire. It was infested by crows and other birds and vultures, all having beaks of iron, as also by evil spirits with long mouths pointed like needles. And it abounded with inaccessible fastnesses like the Vindhya mountains. Human corpses were scattered over it, smeared with fat and blood, with arms and thighs cut off, or with entrails torn out and legs severed.

"'Along that path so disagreeable with the stench of corpses and awful with other incidents, the righteous-souled king proceeded, filled with diverse thoughts. He beheld a river full of boiling water and, therefore, difficult to cross, as also a forest of trees whose leaves were sharp swords and razors. There were plains full of fine white sand exceedingly heated, and rocks and stones made of iron. There were many jars of iron all around, with boiling oil in them. Many a Kuta-salmalika was there, with sharp thorns and, therefore, exceedingly painful to the touch. The son of Kunti beheld also the tortures inflicted upon sinful men.

"'Beholding that inauspicious region abounding with every sort of foulness, Yudhishthira asked the celestial messenger, saying, "How far shall we proceed along a path like this? It behoveth thee to tell me where those brothers of mine are. I desire also to know what region is this of the gods?"

"'Hearing these words of king Yudhishthira the just, the celestial messenger stopped in his course and replied, saying, "Thus far is your way. The denizens of Heaven commanded me that having come thus far, I am to stop. If thou art tired, O king of kings, thou mayst return with me."

"'Yudhishthira, however, was exceedingly disconsolate and stupefied by the foul odour. Resolved to return, O Bharata, he retraced his steps. Afflicted by sorrow and grief, the righteous-souled monarch turned back. Just at that moment he heard piteous lamentations all around, "O son of Dharma, O royal sage, O thou of sacred origin, O son of Pandu, do thou stay a moment for favouring us. At thy approach, O invincible one, a delightful breeze hath begun to blow, bearing the sweet scent of thy person. Great hath been our relief at this. O foremost of kings, beholding thee, O first of men, great hath been our happiness. O son of Pritha, let that happiness last longer through thy stay here, for a few moments more. Do thou remain here, O Bharata, for even a short while. As long as thou art here, O thou of Kuru's race, torments cease to afflict us." These and many similar words, uttered in piteous voices by persons in pain, the king heard in that region, wafted to his ears from every side.

"'Hearing those words of beings in woe, Yudhishthira of compassionate heart exclaimed aloud, "Alas, how painful!" And the king stood still. The speeches of those woe-begone and afflicted persons seemed to the son of Pandu to be uttered in voices that he had heard before although he could not recognise them on that occasion.

"'Unable to recognise voices, Dharma's son, Yudhishthira, enquired, saying,
"Who are you? Why also do you stay here?"

"'Thus addressed, they answered him from all sides, saying, "I am Karna!" "I am Bhimasena!" "I am Arjuna!" "I am Nakula!" "I am Sahadeva!" "I am Dhrishtadyumna!" "I am Draupadi!" "We are the sons of Draupadi!" Even thus, O king, did those voices speak.

"'Hearing those exclamations, O king, uttered in voices of pain suitable to that place, the royal Yudhishthira asked himself, "What perverse destiny is this? What are those sinful acts which were committed by those high-souled beings, Karna and the sons of Draupadi, and the slender-waisted princess of Panchala, so that their residence has been assigned in this region of foetid smell and great woe? I am not aware of any transgression that can be attributed to these persons of righteous deeds. What is that act by doing which Dhritarashtra's son, king Suyodhana, with all his sinful followers, has become invested with such prosperity? Endued with prosperity like that of the great Indra himself, he is highly adored. What is that act through the consequence of which these (high-souled ones) have fallen into Hell? All of them were conversant with every duty, were heroes, were devoted to truth and the Vedas; were observant of Kshatriya practices; were righteous in their acts; were performers of sacrifices; and givers of large presents unto brahmanas. Am I asleep or awake? Am I conscious or unconscious? Or, is all this a mental delusion due to disorders of the brain?"

"'Overwhelmed by sorrow and grief, and with his senses agitated by anxiety, king Yudhishthira indulged in such reflections for a long time. The royal son of Dharma then gave way to great wrath. Indeed, Yudhishthira then censured the gods, as also Dharma himself. Afflicted by the very foul odour, he addressed the celestial messenger, saying, "Return to the presence of those whose messenger thou art. Tell them that I shall not go back to where they are, but shall stay even here, since, in consequence of my companionship, these afflicted brothers of mine have become comforted." Thus addressed by the intelligent son of Pandu, the celestial messenger returned to the place where the chief of the deities was, viz., he of a hundred sacrifices. He represented unto him the acts of Yudhishthira. Indeed, O ruler of men, he informed Indra of all that Dharma's son had said.'"

3

"Vaishampayana said, 'King Yudhishthira the just, the son of Pritha, had not stayed there for more than a moment when, O thou of Kuru's race, all the gods with Indra at their head came to that spot. The deity of Righteousness in his embodied form also came to that place where the Kuru king was, for seeing that monarch. Upon the advent of those deities of resplendent bodies and sanctified and noble deeds, the darkness that had overwhelmed that region immediately disappeared. The torments undergone by beings of sinful deeds were no longer seen. The river Vaitarani, the thorny Salmali, the iron jars, and the boulders of rock, so terrible to behold, also vanished from sight. The diverse repulsive corpses also, which the Kuru king had seen, disappeared at the same time. Then a breeze, delicious and fraught with pleasant perfumes, perfectly pure and delightfully cool, O Bharata, began to blow on that spot in consequence of the presence of the gods. The Maruts, with Indra, the Vasus with the twin Ashvinis, the Sadhyas, the Rudras, the

Adityas, and the other denizens of Heaven, as also the Siddhas and the great Rishis, all came there where Dharma's royal son of great energy was.

"'Then Shakra, the lord of the deities, endued with blazing prosperity, addressed Yudhishthira and comforting him, said, "O Yudhishthira of mighty arms, come, come, O chief of men. These illusions have ended, O puissant one. Success has been attained by thee, O mighty-armed one, and eternal regions (of felicity) have become thine. Thou shouldst not yield to wrath. Listen to these words of mine. Hell, O son, should without doubt be beheld by every king. Of both good and bad there is abundance, O chief of men. He who enjoys first the fruits of his good acts must afterwards endure Hell. He, on the other hand, who first endures Hell, must afterwards enjoy Heaven. He whose sinful acts are many enjoys Heaven first. It is for this, O king, that desirous of doing thee good, I caused thee to be sent for having a view of Hell. Thou hadst, by a pretence, deceived Drona in the matter of his son. Thou hast, in consequence thereof, been shown Hell by an act of deception. After the manner of thyself, Bhima and Arjuna, and Draupadi, have all been shown the place of sinners by an act of deception. Come, O chief of men, all of them have been cleansed of their sins. All those kings who had aided thee and who have been slain in battle, have all attained to Heaven. Come and behold them, O foremost one of Bharata's race.

"'"Karna, the mighty bowman, that foremost of all wielders of weapons for whom thou art grieving, has also attained to high success. Behold, O puissant one, that foremost of men, viz., the son of Surya. He is in that place which is his own, O mighty-armed one. Kill this grief of thine, O chief of men. Behold thy brothers and others, those kings, that is, who had espoused thy side. They have all attained to their respective places (of felicity). Let the fever of thy heart be dispelled. Having endured a little misery first, from this time, O son of Kuru's race, do thou sport with me in happiness, divested of grief and all thy ailments dispelled. O mighty-armed one, do thou now enjoy, O king, the rewards of all thy deeds of righteousness of those regions which thou hast acquired thyself by thy penances and of all thy gifts. Let deities and Gandharvas, and celestial Apsaras, decked in pure robes and excellent ornaments, wait upon and serve thee for thy happiness. Do thou, O mighty-armed one, enjoy now those regions (of felicity) which have become thine through the Rajasuya sacrifice performed by thee and whose felicities have been enhanced by the sacrificial scimitar employed by thee. Let the high fruits of thy penances be enjoyed by thee. Thy regions, O Yudhishthira, are above those of kings. They are equal to those of Hariscandra, O son of Pritha. Come, and sport there in bliss. There where the royal sage Mandhatri is, there where king Bhagiratha is, there where Dushmanta's son Bharata is, there wilt thou sport in bliss. Here is the celestial river, sacred and sanctifying the three worlds. It is called Heavenly Ganga. Plunging into it, thou wilt go to thy own regions. Having bathed in this stream, thou wilt be divested of thy human nature. Indeed, thy grief dispelled, thy ailments conquered, thou wilt be freed from all enmities."

"'While, O Kuru king, the chief of the gods was saying so unto Yudhishthira, the deity of Righteousness, in his embodied form, then addressed his own son and said, "O king, I am greatly pleased, O thou of great wisdom, with thee, O son, by thy devotion to me, by thy truthfulness of speech, and forgiveness, and self-restraint. This, indeed, is the third test, O king, to which I put thee. Thou art incapable, O son of Pritha, of being swerved from thy nature or reason. Before this, I had examined thee in the Dwaita woods by my questions, when thou hadst come to that lake for recovering a couple of fire sticks. Thou stoodst it well. Assuming the shape of a dog, I examined thee once more, O son, when thy brothers with Draupadi had fallen down. This has been thy third test; thou hast expressed thy wish to stay at Hell for the sake of thy brothers. Thou hast become cleansed, O highly blessed one. Purified of sin, be thou happy.

"'"O son of Pritha, thy brothers, O king, were not such as to deserve Hell. All this has been an illusion created by the chief of the gods. Without doubt, all kings, O son, must once behold Hell. Hence hast thou for a little while been subjected to this great affliction. O king, neither Arjuna, nor Bhima, nor any of those foremost of men, viz., the twins, nor Karna, ever truthful in speech and possessed of great courage, could be deserving of Hell for a long time. The princess Krishna too, O Yudhishthira, could not be deserving of that place of sinners. Come, come, O foremost one of the Bharatas, behold Ganga who spreads her current over the three worlds."

"'Thus addressed, that royal sage, viz., thy grandsire, proceeded with Dharma and all the other gods. Having bathed in the celestial river Ganga, sacred and sanctifying and ever adored by the Rishis, he cast off his human body. Assuming then a celestial form, king Yudhishthira the just, in consequence of that bath, became divested of all his enmities and grief. Surrounded by the deities, the Kuru king Yudhishthira then proceeded from that spot. He was accompanied by Dharma, and the great Rishis uttered his praises. Indeed, he reached that place where those foremost of men, those heroes, viz., the Pandavas and the Dhartarashtras, freed from (human) wrath, were enjoying each his respective status.'"

4

"Vaishampayana said, 'King Yudhishthira, thus praised by the gods, the Maruts and the Rishis, proceeded to that place where those foremost ones of Kuru's race were. He beheld Govinda endued with his Brahma-form. It resembled that form of his which had been seen before and which, therefore, helped the recognition. Blazing forth in that form of his, he was adorned with celestial weapons, such as the terrible discus and others in their respective embodied forms. He was being adored by the heroic Phalguna, who also was endued with a blazing effulgence. The son of Kunti beheld the slayer of Madhu also in his own form. Those two foremost of Beings, adored by all the gods, beholding Yudhishthira, received him with proper honours.

"'In another place, the delighter of the Kurus beheld Karna, that foremost one among all wielders of weapons, resembling a dozen Suryas in splendour. In another part he beheld Bhimasena of great puissance, sitting in the midst of the Maruts, and endued with a blazing form. He was sitting by the side of the God of Wind in his embodied form. Indeed, he was then in a celestial form endued with great beauty, and had attained to the highest success. In the place belonging to the Ashvinis, the delighter of the Kurus beheld Nakula and Sahadeva, each blazing with his own effulgence.

"'He also beheld the princess of Panchala, decked in garlands of lotuses. Having attained to Heaven, she was sitting there, endued with a form possessed of solar splendour. King Yudhishthira suddenly wished to question her. Then the illustrious Indra, the chief of the gods, spoke to him, "This one is Sree herself. It was for your sake that she took birth, as the daughter of Drupada, among human beings, issuing not from any mother's womb, O Yudhishthira, endued with agreeable perfume and capable of delighting the whole world. For your pleasure, she was created by the wielder of the trident. She was born in the race of Drupada and was enjoyed by you all. These five highly blessed Gandharvas endued with the effulgence of fire, and possessed of great energy, were, O king, the sons of Draupadi and yourself.

"'"Behold Dhritarashtra, the king of the Gandharvas, possessed of great wisdom. Know that this one was the eldest brother of thy sire. This one is thy eldest brother, the son of Kunti, endued with effulgence of fire. The son of Surya, thy eldest brother, the foremost of men, even this one was known as the son of Radha. He moves in the company of Surya. Behold this foremost of Beings. Among the tribes of the Saddhyas, the gods, the Viswedevas, and the Maruts, behold, O king of kings, the mighty car-warriors of the Vrishnis and the Andhakas, viz., those heroes having Satyaki for their first, and those mighty ones among the Bhojas. Behold the son of Subhadra, invincible in battle, now staying with Soma. Even he is the mighty bowman Abhimanyu, now endued with the gentle effulgence of the great luminary of the night. Here is the mighty bowman Pandu, now united with Kunti and Madri. Thy sire frequently comes to me on his excellent car. Behold the royal Bhishma, the son of Santanu, now in the midst of the Vasus. Know that this one by the side of Brihaspati is thy preceptor Drona. These and other kings, O son of Pandu, who had warred on thy side now walk with the Gandharvas or Yakshas or other sacred beings. Some have attained to the status of Guhyakas, O king. Having cast off their bodies, they have conquered Heaven by the merit they had acquired through word, thought and deed.'"'

5

"Janamejaya said, 'Bhishma and Drona, those two high-souled persons, king Dhritarashtra, and Virata and Drupada, and Sankha and Uttara, Dhrishtaketu and Jayatsena and king Satyajit, the sons of Duryodhana, and Shakuni the son of Subala, Karna's sons of great prowess, king Jayadratha, Ghatotkaca and others whom thou hast not mentioned, the other heroic kings of blazing forms, tell me for what period they remained in Heaven. O foremost of regenerate persons, was theirs an eternal place in Heaven? What was the end attained to by those foremost of men when their acts came to an end? I desire to hear this, O foremost of regenerate persons, and therefore have I asked thee. Through thy blazing penances thou seest all things."'

Sauti said: "Thus questioned, that regenerate Rishi, receiving the permission of the high-souled Vyasa, set himself to answer the question of the king.

"Vaishampayana said, 'Every one, O king of men, is not capable of returning to his own nature at the end of his deeds. Whether this is so or not, is, indeed a good question asked by thee. Hear, O king, this which is a mystery of the gods, O chief of Bharata's race. It was explained (to us) by Vyasa of mighty energy, celestial vision and great prowess, that ancient ascetic, O Kauravya, who is the son of Parasara and who always observes high vows, who is of immeasurable understanding, who is omniscient, and who, therefore knows the end attached to all acts.

"'Bhishma of mighty energy and great effulgence attained to the status of the Vasus. Eight Vasus, O chief of Bharata's race, are now seen. Drona entered into Brihaspati, that foremost one of Angirasa's descendants. Hridika's son Kritavarma entered the Maruts. Pradyumna entered Sanatkumara whence he had issued. Dhritarashtra obtained the regions, so difficult of acquisition, that belong to the Lord of treasures. The famous Gandhari obtained the same regions with her husband Dhritarashtra. With his two wives, Pandu proceeded to the abode of the great Indra. Both Virata and Drupada, the king Dhrishtaketu, as also Nishatha, Akrura, Samva, Bhanukampa, and Viduratha, and Bhurishrava and Sala and king Bhuri, and Kansa, and

Ugrasena, and Vasudeva, and Uttara, that foremost of men, with his brother Sankha, all these foremost of persons entered the deities. Soma's son of great prowess, named Varchas of mighty energy, became Abhimanyu, the son of Phalguna, that lion among men. Having fought, agreeably to Kshatriya practices, with bravery such as none else had ever been able to show, that mighty-armed and righteous-souled being entered Soma. Slain on the field of battle, O foremost of men, Karna entered Surya. Shakuni obtained absorption into Dwapara, and Dhrishtadyumna into the deity of fire. The sons of Dhritarashtra were all Rakshasas of fierce might. Sanctified by death caused by weapons, those high-souled beings of prosperity all succeeded in attaining to Heaven. Both Kshattri and king Yudhishthira entered into the god of Righteousness. The holy and illustrious Ananta (who had taken birth as Balarama) proceeded to the region below the Earth. Through the command of the Grandsire, he, aided by his Yoga power, supported the Earth. Vasudeva was a portion of that eternal god of gods called Narayana. Accordingly, he entered into Narayana. 16,000 women had been married to Vasudeva as his wives. When the time came, O Janamejaya, they plunged into the Sarasvati. Casting off their (human) bodies there, they re-ascended to Heaven. Transformed into Apsaras, they approached the presence of Vasudeva. Those heroic and mighty car-warriors, Ghatotkaca and others, who were slain in the great battle, attained to the status, some of gods and some of Yakshas. Those that had fought on the side of Duryodhana are said to have been Rakshasas. Gradually, O king, they have all attained to excellent regions of felicity. Those foremost of men have proceeded, some to the abode of Indra, some to that of Kuvera of great intelligence, and some to that of Varuna. I have now told thee, O thou of great splendour, everything about the acts, O Bharata, of both the Kurus and the Pandavas.'"

Sauti said: "Hearing this, ye foremost of regenerate ones, at the intervals of sacrificial rites, king Janamejaya became filled with wonder. The sacrificial priests then finished the rites that remained to be gone through. Astika, having rescued the snakes (from fiery death), became filled with joy. King Janamejaya then gratified all the Brahmanas with copious presents. Thus worshipped by the king, they returned to their respective abodes. Having dismissed those learned Brahmanas, king Janamejaya came back from Takshasila to the city named after the elephant.

"I have now told everything that Vaishampayana narrated, at the command of Vyasa, unto the king at his snake sacrifice. Called a history, it is sacred, sanctifying and excellent. It has been composed by the ascetic Krishna, O Brahmana, of truthful speech. He is omniscient, conversant with all ordinances, possessed of a knowledge of all duties, endued with piety, capable of perceiving what is beyond the ken of the senses, pure, having a soul cleansed by penances, possessed of the six high attributes, and devoted to Sankhya Yoga. He has composed this, beholding everything with a celestial eye that has been cleansed (strengthened) by varied lore. He has done this, desiring to spread the fame, throughout the world, of the high-souled Pandavas, as also of other Kshatriyas possessed of abundant wealth of energy.

"That learned man who recites this history of sacred days in the midst of a listening auditory becomes cleansed of every sin, conquers Heaven, and attains to the status of Brahma. Of that man who listens with rapt attention to the recitation of the whole of this Veda composed by (the Island-born) Krishna, a million sins, numbering such grave ones as Brahmanicide and the rest, are washed off. The Pitris of that man who recites even a small portion of this history at a Sraddha, obtain inexhaustible food and drink. The sins that one commits during the day by one's senses or the mind are all washed off before evening by reciting a portion of the Mahabharata. Whatever sins a Brahmana may commit at night in the midst of women are all washed off before dawn by reciting a portion of the Mahabharata.

"The high race of the Bharatas is its topic. Hence it is called Bharata. And because of its grave import, as also of the Bharatas being its topic, it is called Mahabharata. He who is versed in interpretations of this great treatise, becomes cleansed of every sin. Such a man lives in righteousness, wealth, and pleasure, and attains to Emancipation also, O chief of Bharata's race.

"That which occurs here occurs elsewhere. That which does not occur here occurs nowhere else. This history is known by the name of Jaya. It should be heard by every one desirous of Emancipation. It should be read by Brahmanas, by kings, and by women quick with children. He that desires Heaven attains to Heaven; and he that desires victory attains to victory. The woman quick with child gets either a son or a daughter highly blessed. The puissant Island-born Krishna, who will not have to come back, and who is Emancipation incarnate, made an abstract of the Bharata, moved by the desire of aiding the cause of righteousness. He made another compilation consisting of sixty lakhs of verses. Thirty lakhs of these were placed in the region of the deities. In the region of the Pitris fifteen lakhs, it should be known, are current; while in that of the Yakshas fourteen lakhs are in vogue. One lakh is current among human beings.

"Narada recited the Mahabharata to the gods; Asita-Devala to the Pitris; Suka to the Rakshasas and the Yakshas; and Vaishampayana to human beings. This history is sacred, and of high import, and regarded as equal to the Vedas. That man, O Saunaka, who hears this history, placing a

Brahmana before him, acquires both fame and the fruition of all his wishes. He who, with fervid devotion, listens to a recitation of the Mahabharata, attains (hereafter) to high success in consequence of the merit that becomes his through understanding even a very small portion thereof. All the sins of that man who recites or listens to this history with devotion are washed off.

"In former times, the great Rishi Vyasa, having composed this treatise, caused his son Suka to read it with him, along with these four Verses. Thousands of mothers and fathers, and hundreds of sons and wives arise in the world and depart from it. Others will (arise and) similarly depart. There are thousands of occasions for joy and hundreds of occasions for fear. These affect only him that is ignorant but never him that is wise. With uplifted arms I am crying aloud but nobody hears me. From Righteousness is Wealth as also Pleasure. Why should not Righteousness, therefore, be courted? For the sake neither of pleasure, nor of fear, nor of cupidity should any one cast off Righteousness. Indeed, for the sake of even life one should not cast off Righteousness. Righteousness is eternal. Pleasure and Pain are not eternal. Jiva is eternal. The cause, however, of Jiva's being invested with a body is not so.

"That man who, waking up at dawn, reads this Savittri of the Bharata, acquires all the rewards attached to a recitation of this history and ultimately attains to the highest Brahma. As the sacred Ocean, as the Himavat mountain, are both regarded as mines of precious gems, even so is this Bharata (regarded as a mine of precious gems). The man of learning, by reciting to others this Veda or Agama composed by (the Island-born) Krishna, earns wealth. There is no doubt in this that he who, with rapt attention, recites this history called Bharata, attains to high success. What need has that man of a sprinkling of the waters of Pushkara who attentively listens to this Bharata, while it is recited to him? It represents the nectar that fell from the lips of the Island-born. It is immeasurable, sacred, sanctifying, sin-cleansing, and auspicious."

6

"Janamejaya said, 'O holy one, according to what rites should the learned listen to the Bharata? What are the fruits (acquirable by hearing it)? What deities are to be worshipped during the several paranas? What should be the gifts that one should make, O holy one, at every parva or sacred day (during the continuance of the recitation)? What should be the qualification of the reciter to be engaged? Tell me all this!'

"Vaishampayana said, 'Hear, O king, what the procedure is, and what the fruits, O Bharata, are that will spring from ones listening (to a recitation of the Bharata). Even this, O king of kings, is what thou askest me. The deities of Heaven, O ruler of Earth, came to this world for sport. Having achieved their task, they ascended once more to Heaven. Listen to what I shall tell thee in brief. In the Mahabharata is to be found the births of Rishis and deities on the Earth. In this treatise, called Bharata, O foremost one of Bharata's race, are to be seen in one place the eternal Rudras, the Saddhyas, and the Viswedevas; the Adityas, the two deities named the Ashvinis, the regents of the World, the great Rishis, the Guhyakas, the Gandharvas, the Nagas, the Vidyadharas, the Siddhas, the diverse deities, the Self-born visible in a body, with many ascetics; the Hills and Mountains, Oceans and Seas and Rivers, the diverse tribes of Apsaras; the Planets, the Years, the Half-years, and the Seasons; and the whole universe of mobile and immobile entities, with all the gods and Asuras.

"'Hearing their celebrity, and in consequence of a recitation of their names and achievements, a man that has committed even terrible sins, will be cleansed. Having, with a concentrated soul and cleansed body, heard this history duly, from the beginning, and having reached its end, one should make Sraddha offerings, O Bharata, unto those (foremost of persons who have been mentioned in it). Unto the Brahmanas also, O chief of Bharata's race, should, with due devotion and according to ones power, be made large gifts and diverse kinds of gems, and kine, and vessels of white brass for milking kine, and maidens decked with every ornament, and possessed of every accomplishment suited to enjoyment, as also diverse kinds of conveyances, beautiful mansions, plots of land, and cloths. Animals also should be given, such as horses and elephants in rage, and beds, and covered conveyances borne on the shoulders of men, and well-decked cars. Whatever objects occur in the house, of the foremost kind, whatever wealth of great value occurs in it, should be given away unto Brahmanas. Indeed, one should give away one's own self, wives, and children.

"'One desirous of hearing the Bharata, should hear it without a doubting heart, with cheerfulness and joy; and as he proceeds listening to its recitation, he should according to the extent of his power, make gifts with great devotion.

"'Hear how a person that is devoted to truth and sincerity, that is self-restrained, pure (in mind), and observant of those acts which lead to purity of body, that is endued with faith, and that has subjugated wrath, attains to success (in the matter of a recitation of the Bharata). He should appoint as reciter one that is pure (of body), that is endued with good and pious conduct, that should be robed in white, that should have a complete mastery over his passions, that is cleansed of all offences, that is conversant with every branch of learning, that is endued with faith, that is free from malice, that is possessed of handsome features, that is blessed, self-restrained, truthful, and with passions under control, and that is beloved of all for the gifts he makes and the honours of which he is the possessor.

"'The reciter, seated at his ease, free from all bodily complaints, and with rapt attention, should recite the text without too much slowness, without a labouring voice, without being fast or quick, quietly, with sufficient energy, without confusing the letters and words together, in a sweet intonation and with such accent and emphasis as would indicate the sense giving full utterance to the three and sixty letters of the alphabet from the eight places of their formation. Bowing unto Narayana, and to Nara, that foremost of men, as also to the goddess Sarasvati, should the word Jaya be uttered.

"'Listening to the Bharata, O king, when recited, O thou of Bharata's race, by a reader of this kind, the listener, observant of vows all the while and cleansed by purificatory rites, acquires valuable fruits. When the first Parana is reached, the hearer should gratify Brahmanas with presents of all desirable objects. By doing this, one obtains the fruits of the Agnishtoma sacrifice. He acquires a large (celestial) car teeming with diverse orders of Apsaras (that wait upon him). With a glad heart, and with the deities in his company, he proceeds to Heaven, his heart rapt (in felicity).

"'When the second Parana is reached, the hearer acquires the fruits of the Atiratra vow. Indeed, he ascends a celestial car made entirely of precious gems. Wearing celestial garlands and robes, and decked with celestial unguents and always shedding a celestial fragrance around, he receives high honours in Heaven.

"'When the third Parana is reached, he acquires the fruits of the Dwadasaha vow. Indeed he resides in Heaven for myriads of years, like a god.

"'At the fourth Parana he acquires the fruits of the Vajapeya sacrifice.

"'At the fifth, twice those fruits are his. Ascending a celestial car that resembles the rising sun or a blazing fire, and with the deities for his companions, he goes to Heaven and sports in felicity for myriads of years in the abode of Indra.

"'At the sixth Parana, twice, and at the seventh, thrice those fruits become his. Ascending a celestial car that resembles the summit of the

Kailasa mountains (in beauty), that is equipt with an altar made of stones of lapis lazuli and other precious gems, that is surrounded by beautiful objects of diverse kinds, that is decked with gems and corals, that moves at the will of the rider, and that teems with waiting Apsaras, he roves through all the regions of felicity, like a second deity of the Sun.

"'At the eight Parana, he acquires the fruits of the Rajasuya sacrifice. He ascends a car as beautiful as the rising moon, and unto which are yoked steeds white as the rays of the moon and endued with the speed of thought. He is served by women of the foremost beauty and whose faces are more charming than the moon. He hears the music of the garlands that encircle their waists and the Nupuras encircling their ankles. Sleeping with his head resting on the laps of women of transcendent beauty, he awakes greatly refreshed.

"'At the ninth Parana, he acquires, O Bharata, the fruits of that foremost of sacrifices, viz., the Horse-sacrifice. Ascending on a car equipt with a chamber consisting of a top supported by columns of gold, furnished with a seat made of stones of lapis lazuli, with windows on all sides made of pure gold, and teeming with waiting Apsaras and Gandharvas and other celestials, he blazes forth in splendour. Wearing celestial garlands and robes, and decked with celestial unguents, he sports in bliss, with deities for his companions, in Heaven, like a second deity himself.

"'Reaching the tenth Parana and gratifying Brahmanas, he acquires a car which tinkles with innumerable bells, which is decked with flags and banners, which is equipt with a seat made of precious gems, which has many arches made of lapis lazuli, which has a net-work of gold all round, which has turrets made of corals, which is adorned with Gandharvas and Apsaras well-skilled in singing, and which is fit for the residence of the Righteous. Crowned with a diadem of the complexion of fire, decked with ornaments of gold, his person smeared with celestial sandal paste, garnished with celestial wreaths, he roves through all celestial regions, enjoying all celestial objects of enjoyment, and endued with great splendour, through the grace of the deities.

"'Thus accoutred, he receives high honours in Heaven for many long years. With Gandharvas in his company, for full 21,000 years, he sports in bliss with Indra himself in abode of Indra. He roves at pleasure every day through the diverse regions of the gods, riding on celestial cars and conveyances, and surrounded by celestial damsels of transcendent beauty. He is able to go to the abode of the solar deity, of the lunar deity, and of Siva, O king. Indeed, he succeeds in living in the same region with Vishnu himself. It is even so, O monarch. There is no doubt in this. A person listening with faith, becomes even so. My preceptor has said this. Unto the reciter should be given all such objects as he may wish. Elephants and steeds and cars and conveyances, especially animals and the vehicles they draw, a bracelet of gold, a pair of ear-rings, sacred threads, beautiful robes, and perfumes in especial (should be given). By worshipping him as a deity one attains to the regions of Vishnu.

"'After this I shall declare what should be given away, as each parva is reached of the Bharata in course of its recitation, unto brahmanas, after ascertaining their birth, country, truthfulness, and greatness, O chief of Bharata's race, as also their inclination for piety, and unto Kshatriyas too, O king, after ascertainment of similar particulars. Causing the Brahmanas to utter benedictions, the business of recitation should be begun. When a parva is finished, the brahmanas should be worshipped to the best of one's power. At first, the reciter, clad in good robes and smeared with perfumed paste, should, O king, be duly fed with honey and frumenty of the best kind.

"'When the Astika-parva is being recited, brahmanas should be entertained with fruits and roots, and frumenty, and honey and clarified butter, and rice boiled with raw sugar.

"'When the Sabha-parva is being recited, brahmanas should be fed with habisya along with apupas and pupas and modakas, O king.

"'When the Aranyaka-parva is being recited, superior brahmanas should be fed with fruits and roots.

"'When the Arani-parva is reached, water-pots full of water should be given away. Many superior kinds of delicious food, also rice and fruits and roots, and food possessed of every agreeable attribute, should be presented unto the brahmanas.

"'During the recitation of the Virata-parva diverse kinds of robes should be given away; and during that of the Udyoga-parva, O chief of the Bharatas, the twice-born ones, after being decked with perfumes and garlands, should be entertained with food possessed of every agreeable quality.

"'During the recitation of the Bhishma-parva, O king of kings, after giving them excellent cars and conveyances, food should be given that is pure and well-cooked and possessed of every desirable attribute.

"'During the Drona-parva food of very superior kind should be given to learned brahmanas, as also beds, O monarch, and bows and good swords.

"'During the recitation of the Karna-parva, food of the foremost kind, besides being pure and well-cooked, should be presented unto the brahmanas by the house-holder with rapt mind.

"'During the recitation of the Shalya-parva, O king of kings, food with confectionery and rice boiled with raw sugar, as also cakes of wheat and soothing and nutritive viands and drinks should be presented.

"'During the recitation of the Gada-parva, brahmanas should be entertained with food mixed with mudga.

"'During the recitation of the Stri-parva, foremost of brahmanas should be entertained with gems and precious stones; and during the recitation of the Aishika-parva, rice boiled in ghee should first be given, and then food pure and well-cooked, and possessed of every desirable quality, should be presented.

"'During the recitation of the Shanti-parva, the brahmanas should be fed with havisya.

"'When the Asvamedhika-parva is reached, food possessed of every agreeable quality should be given; and when the Asramvasika is reached, brahmanas should be entertained with havisya.

"'When the Mausala is reached, scents and garlands possessed of agreeable qualities should be given away.

"'During the Mahaprasthanika, similar presents should be made, possessed of every quality of an agreeable kind.

"'When the Svarga-parva is reached, the brahmanas should be fed with havisya.

"'Upon the conclusion of the Harivansa, a 1,000 brahmanas should be fed. Unto each of them should be presented a cow accompanied with a piece of gold. Half of this should be presented to each poor man, O king.

"'Upon the conclusion of all the Parvas, the house-holder of wisdom should give unto the reciter a copy of the Mahabharata with a piece of gold. When the Harivansa Parva is being recited, Brahmanas should be fed with frumenty at each successive Parana, O king. Having finished all the Parvas, one versed in the scriptures, robing himself in white, wearing garlands, decked with ornaments, and properly purified, should place a copy of the Mahabharata on an auspicious spot and cover it with a piece of silken cloth and worship it, according to due rites, with scents and garlands, offering each at a time. Indeed, O king, the several volumes of this treatise should be worshipped by one with devotion and concentrated mind. Offerings should be made unto them of diverse kinds of food and garlands and drinks and diverse auspicious articles of enjoyment. Gold and other precious metals should be given as Dakshina. The names should then be taken of all the deities as also of Nara and Narayana. Then, adorning the persons of some foremost of Brahmanas with scents and garlands, they should be gratified with diverse kinds of gifts of enjoyable and very superior or costly articles. By doing this, one attains to the merits of the Atiratra sacrifice. Indeed, at each successive Parva, he acquires the merits that attach to the performance of a sacrifice. The reciter, O chief of the Bharatas, should be possessed of learning and endued with a good voice and a clear utterance respecting both letters and words. Even such a man should, O chief of the Bharatas, recite the Bharata. After entertaining a number of foremost Brahmanas, presents should be made unto them according to the ordinances. The reciter also, O chief of the Bharatas, should be decked with ornaments and fed sumptuously. The reciter being gratified, the house-holder attains to an excellent and auspicious contentment. If the Brahmanas are gratified, all the deities are gratified. After this, O chief of the Bharatas, Brahmanas should be duly entertained with diverse kinds of enjoyable articles and superior things.

"'I have thus indicated the ordinances, O foremost of men, (about the manner of reciting these scriptures) in answer to thy enquiries. Thou shouldst observe them with faith. In listening to a recitation of the Bharata and at each Parana, O best of kings, one that desires to attain to the highest good should listen with the greatest care and attention. One should listen to the Bharata every day. One should proclaim the merits of the Bharata every day. One in whose house the Bharata occurs, has in his hands all those scriptures which are known by the name of Jaya. The Bharata is cleansing and sacred. In the Bharata are diverse topics. The Bharata is worshipped by the very gods. The Bharata is the highest goal. The Bharata, O chief of the Bharatas, is the foremost of all scriptures. One attains to Emancipation through the Bharata. This that I tell thee is certain truth. One that proclaims the merits of this history called the Mahabharata, of the Earth, of the cow, of Sarasvati (the goddess of speech), of Brahmanas, and of Keshava, has never to languish.

"'In the Vedas, in the Ramayana, and in the sacred Bharata, O chief of Bharata's race, Hari is sung in the beginning, the middle, and at the end. That in which occur excellent statements relating to Vishnu, and the eternal Srutis, should be listened to by men desirous of attaining to the highest goal. This treatise is sanctifying. This is the highest indicator as regards duties; this is endued with every merit. One desirous of prosperity should listen to it. Sins committed by means of the body, by means of words, and by means of the mind, are all destroyed (through listening to the Bharata) as Darkness at sunrise. One devoted to Vishnu acquires (through this) that merit which is acquired by listening to the eighteen Puranas. There is no doubt in this. Men and women (by listening to this) would certainly attain to the status of Vishnu. Women desirous of having children should certainly listen to this which proclaims the fame of Vishnu. One desirous of attaining to the fruits that attach to a recitation of the Bharata should, according to one's power, give unto the reciter Dakshina, as also an honorarium in gold. One desirous of one's own good should give unto the reciter a Kapila cow with horns cased in gold and accompanied by her calf, covered with a cloth. Ornaments, O chief of Bharatas race, for the arms, as also those for the ears, should be given. Besides these, other kinds of wealth should be presented. Unto the reciter, O king of men, gift of land should be made. No gift like that of land could ever be or will be. The man that listens (to the Bharata) or that recites it to other people, becomes cleansed of all his sins and attains at last to the status of Vishnu. Such a man rescues his ancestors to the eleventh degree, as also himself with his wives and sons, O chief of Bharata's race. After concluding a recitation of the Bharata, one should, O king, perform a Homa with all its ten parts.

"'I have thus, O chief of men, told everything in thy presence. He that listens with devotion to this Bharata from the beginning becomes cleansed of every sin even if he be guilty of Brahmanicide or the violation of his preceptor's bed, or even if he be a drinker of alcohol or a robber of other people's wares, or even if he be born in the Chandala order. Destroying all his sins like the maker of day destroying darkness, such a man, without doubt, sports in felicity in the region of Vishnu like Vishnu himself.'"

The End of the Svargarohanika-parva

The Eighteen parvas of the Mahabharata are thus complete.